T0344581

MIRI LEE

VERY

PERSON

avedition

V.I.P.
VERY IMPORTANT PERSON.

IS THE PERSON REALLY IMPORTANT?
EVEN MORE IMPORTANT THAN SOMEONE ELSE?

WHAT DOES V.I.P. REALLY STAND FOR?

VERY

I

PERSON

VERY

INCORRECT

PERSON

BRAIN

VERY

IGNORANT

PERSON

VERY

INFAMOUS

PERSON

VERY

INSPIRED

PERSON

VERY

INSURED

PERSON

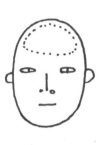

VERY

INNOCENT

PERSON

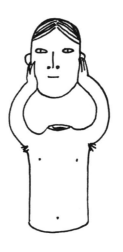

VERY

IMPOSSIBLE

PERSON

VERY

INCAPACITATED

PERSON

VERY

INSECURE

PERSON

VERY

INSOCIABLE

PERSON

VERY

ILL

PERSON

VERY

INTENSE

PERSON

VERY

IMPATIENT

PERSON

VERY

IMMORAL

PERSON

VERY

ISOLATED

PERSON

VERY

IRRITATING

PERSON

VERY

INTENSIVE

PERSON

VERY
IDOLIZED
PERSON

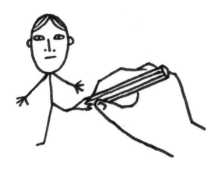

VERY
INCOMPLETE
PERSON

VERY
ILLEGAL
PERSON

$ $ $

VERY

INSANE

PERSON

VERY

INTOXICATED

PERSON

VERY

IRRESPONSIBLE

PERSON

VERY

INFECTED

PERSON

VERY

IMMORTAL

PERSON

VERY

INSISTENT

PERSON

VERY

INGENIOUS

PERSON

VERY

IMPRISONED

PERSON

Mr.

Google

VERY

INTELLIGENT

PERSON

VERY   ILL

ARY   PERSON

VERY

INTOLERANT

PERSON

VERY

IDEAL

PERSON

VERY
ILL-MANNERED
PERSON

VERY

INDEFENSIBLE

PERSON

VERY

IDIOTIC

PERSON

VERY

IMITATED

PERSON

VERY
INVISIBLE
PERSON

VERY
INTERESTING
PERSON

VERY

INDESCRIBABLE

PERSON

VERY

INDIFFERENT

PERSON

VERY
INJURIOUS
PERSON

VERY

ITALIAN

PERSON

VERY

IMPRESSIVE

PERSON

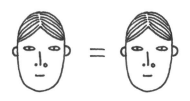

VERY

IDENTICAL

PERSON

VERY
INBORN
PERSON

VERY

INGLORIOUS

PERSON

VERY

ITCHY

PERSON

VERY

INCONSIDERATE

PERSON

VERY

INSENSITIVE

PERSON

VERY

INSTINCTIVE

PERSON

VERY

IDENTIFIED

PERSON

VERY

INCREDIBLE

PERSON

VERY

INNOVATIVE

PERSON

VERY

IN LOVE

PERSON

VERY

IMPORTANT

PERSONALITY

IT DOESN'T MATTER
WHAT YOU LOOK LIKE.

IT DOESN'T MATTER
WHAT YOU HAVE.

IT DOESN'T MATTER
WHAT YOU DO.

IT DOESN'T MATTER
WHO YOU ARE.

YOU ARE IMPORTANT.

IMPRINT

CONCEPT, ILLUSTRATIONS & TEXTS

MIRI LEE
WWW.MIRILEE.DE

COPYRIGHT 2015

MIRI LEE, KONSTANZ

DISTRIBUTION

AV EDITION GMBH, STUTTGART
PUBLISHERS FOR ARCHITECTURE AND DESIGN
WWW.AVEDITION.COM

ISBN 978-3-89986-224-9
PRINTED IN GERMANY

PRINTING

KÖSEL GMBH & CO. KG
WWW.KOESELBUCH.DE

COOPERATION

A SERIES OF DESIGN STUDENT PROJECTS FOR
THE 2015 YEAR OF JUSTICE IN CONSTANCE
WWW.KD.HTWG-KONSTANZ.DE

Konzilstadt
Konstanz

DESIGNER FÜR GERECHTIGKEIT

HOCHSCHULE
KONSTANZ
TECHNIK, WIRTSCHAFT
UND GESTALTUNG